PET DOGS

Teresa Pritlove

Grolier
an imprint of

SCHOLASTIC

www.scholastic.com/librarypublishing

Published 2009 by Grolier
An Imprint of Scholastic Library Publishing
Old Sherman Turnpike
Danbury, Connecticut 06816

For The Brown Reference Group plc
Project Editor: Jolyon Goddard
Picture Researchers: Clare Newman, Sophie
Mortimer
Designer: Sarah Williams
Managing Editor: Tim Harris

Volume ISBN-13: 978-0-7172-8048-3
Volume ISBN-10: 0-7172-8048-9

**Library of Congress
Cataloging-in-Publication Data**

Nature's children. Set 5.
    p. cm.
  Includes index.
  ISBN-13: 978-0-7172-8084-1
  ISBN-10: 0-7172-8084-5 (set)
  1. Animals--Encyclopedias, Juvenile. I.
Grolier Educational (Firm)
  QL49.N386 2009
  590.3--dc22
                        2008014674

Printed and bound in China

PICTURE CREDITS

Front cover: **Shutterstock**: Carlos Arranz.

Back cover: **Shutterstock:** Andreas Gradin,
Jack, Scrivener, Jennifer Sekerka, Vahamrick.

Getty Images: LWA/Larry Williams 37,
Andy Sacks/Stone 30; **Rex Features**: Sam
Barcroft 33; **Shutterstock**: 41, Carlos
Arranz 17, Alexey Avdev 21, Anna Dzondzua
45, Natalia V. Guseva 2–3, 22, Illustionstudio
42, Eric Isselée 4, 5, Gail Johnson 13, Ingvaid
Kaldhussater 10, Katrina Leigh 6, Iztok Noc
46, Pavitra 38, pixshots 18, 26–27, plastique 9,
Magdalena Szachowska 14, 34, Jan de Wild 29.

Contents

Fact File: Pet Dogs 4

Lasting Friends 7

Canid Cousins 8

Pedigree or Pooch? 11

Sporting Dogs 12

Hounds 15

Terriers 16

Toy Dogs 19

Working Dogs 20

Nonsporting Dogs 23

Herding Dogs 24

A Friend for Life 25

Feature Photo 26–27

Puppy Love 28

Making Friends 31

Who's in Charge? 32

House-training 35

A Visit to the Vet 36

Favorite Foods 39

In the Doghouse. 40

Keeping Clean. 43

Fun and Games. 44

Showing Off 47

Dog Stars. 48

Words to Know 49

Find Out More 51

Index. 52

FACT FILE: Pet Dogs

Class	Mammals (Mammalia)
Order	Carnivores (Carnivora)
Family	Dog family (Canidae)
Genus	Wolves, coyotes, jackals, and dogs (*Canis*)
Species	Gray wolf, dingo, and domestic dog (*C. lupus*)
Subspecies	Domestic dog (*C. l. familiaris*)
World distribution	Native throughout the world, except on remote islands and in Australia, where they were brought in by humans
Habitat	Found alongside people in most habitats, including forests, deserts, polar and mountainous areas, and cities
Distinctive physical characteristics	All dogs walk on their toes; have strong jaws and sharp teeth, especially canine teeth
Habits	Live as a group, or pack, with one dominant dog; pet dogs often think of human families as packs
Diet	Mostly meat, but also fish, cereals, cooked vegetables, and certain fruits

Introduction

Dogs have been around for many thousands of years. Over the centuries, they have become helpful to people in many ways. Dogs can hunt, herd sheep and cows, pull heavy loads, and guard people and property. And because they are loyal companions, they make great pets.

Today there are more **breeds**, or kinds, of dogs than any other **domestic**, or tame, animal. They can all make wonderful pets, whatever the breed. As pets, dogs need a lot of love and attention. But the reward for all that care is a lifelong friend!

Basset hounds were first bred in France.

Sheepdogs are considered to be very intelligent dogs. There are many different breeds, and they also make good pets.

Lasting Friends

Dogs are very good at hunting and herding. That is probably why they were one of the first wild animals to be domesticated. Stone Age cave paintings and ancient statues show them hunting alongside their human masters. Later civilizations, such as the ancient Greeks and Egyptians, also used dogs to help them hunt and round up goats and sheep.

Some modern dogs are still used for hunting and herding—among other important jobs. Sniffer dogs have a highly sensitive nose and are trained to detect bombs or illegal drugs. Rescue dogs are good swimmers and save people from drowning. Others entertain us in shows, competitions, dog races, and circuses. Some are even television and movie stars!

Dogs have been useful servants since prehistoric times. However, most owners today simply value their dogs for their friendship and companionship.

Canid Cousins

Dogs and wolves are closely related. They both belong to a group, or family, of **mammals** called the Canids (KA-NIDS), which is the scientific name for the dog family. In fact, wolves are thought to be the wild **ancestors** of dogs. Domestic dogs probably came about when cave dwellers adopted wolf cubs. These cubs would have grown up around humans and become friendly and helpful.

Dogs now come in all shapes and sizes. Some, such as Siberian huskies, are still very similar to wolves. However, other dogs, such as a tiny Chihuahua (CHU-WA-WA), look nothing at all like a wolf!

Humans started choosing which dogs to breed according to how helpful they were or for their size and shape. Some breeds, therefore, became better at certain tasks than others. For example, huskies are strong and can be used for pulling sleds, but a toy poodle would be no good as a police dog!

Huskies are strong dogs
bred to pull sleds.

The Leonburger is a large dog that originates from Germany. It was bred from three types of dogs—the Newfoundland, Saint Bernard, and Pyrenean mountain dog.

Pedigree or Pooch?

Today in the United States, there are more than 150 breeds of dogs officially recognized, or **registered**. A registered purebred dog is called a **pedigree**. Each pedigree belongs to one of seven groups—sporting, hound, working, terrier, toy, nonsporting, or herding dogs.

Though not pedigrees, there are countless other kinds of dogs. Many dogs are a mixture of two breeds—these are called **crossbreeds**. The gentle, good-natured Labrador retrievers have been recently crossed with poodles. Unlike Labradors, poodles do not shed their fur. The result was a new breed called the "Labradoodle," a gentle dog that does not leave hair everywhere!

Many people prefer **mongrels**, or mutts, a mixture of various breeds. Mutts tend to be tougher and less likely to have diseases. They often have a personality all of their own—because they have not been bred to be helpful to people!

Sporting Dogs

Pointers, setters, retrievers, and spaniels are all types of sporting dogs. They were bred and trained over many centuries to help hunters catch wild **prey** by sniffing out the prey's hiding places.

Pointers and setters use their nose to point toward prey so the hunter can then find it. Pet pointers and setters love to play hide-and-go-seek—although they are much better at seeking than hiding! Retrievers happily charge across fields or jump into water to fetch prey. They love to leap into a pond or lake after anything—even a stone thrown by their owner. Spaniels **flush** prey from their hiding places in bushes or long grass. A pet spaniel might chase a squirrel up a tree and sit on guard beneath it—just in case the squirrel loses its balance!

A retriever is bred and trained to bring back shot ducks to its owner without damaging them.

13

Basenjis (BUH-**SEN**-JEEZ) weigh up to 24 pounds (11 kg). Breeds such as the basenji are known as square dogs because they are as long as they are tall.

Hounds

Like sporting dogs, hounds were bred for hunting. Some have sharp eyes, others have a keen nose, some have great strength or endurance, and others are very fast runners.

Scent hounds use their highly developed sense of smell to **track** prey. A bloodhound can follow a scent that is many days old. Sight, or gaze, hounds have sharp eyesight, which they use to spot prey, often from a great distance.

The basenji, an ancient breed, is a sight hound that combines sight, pointing, retrieving, and racing skills to hunt. The ancient Egyptians valued these dogs. Carvings found in the tombs of the pharaohs show basenjis sitting at the feet of their masters. The only thing a basenji cannot do is bark, which makes it a good pet for people who dislike yappy dogs. Instead, it gives out a whine that sounds like a soft yodel.

Terriers

Terriers love to dig holes. These tough little dogs were originally bred to hunt vermin, such as weasels, groundhogs, and rats, by digging them out of their hiding places in the ground. With fierce determination—and very strong jaws—terriers can hold onto the vermin until the hunter arrives.

Most terriers are small and stocky, like the bull terrier or the Boston terrier. But some are much bigger. The largest breed of terrier is the Airedale, which can be up to 2 feet (60 cm) tall at the shoulders. Terriers make good guard dogs because they are brave and determined. They also make excellent family pets because they are loyal and affectionate. They have a lot of personality, too, which makes them great fun!

Yorkshire terriers, or "Yorkies," are small terriers that were developed to catch rats. They are now one of the most popular breeds of pet dogs in the United States.

Chihuahuas are the smallest breed of dog, measuring up to 9 inches (23 cm) at the shoulders. They originate from Mexico.

Toy Dogs

There are several breeds of toy dogs. Some of the most unusual-looking dogs in the world fall into this group. Unusual-looking or not, they all have one thing in common: they are all very small!

Toy dogs were most likely developed by people who only wanted dogs as pets. These dogs were very popular with wealthy ladies, who would often hold the dogs in their lap to keep themselves warm. Many famous paintings show toy dogs curled up on the end of a bed keeping the occupant's feet warm!

Some toy dogs, such as toy poodles, are just smaller versions of a larger breed. Others, such as pugs, are distinct breeds of their own. Pugs are the largest toy dogs, and they can weigh up to 18 pounds (8.2 kg).

The toy breeds are all very popular. They make very good pets because they are easy to control, and they eat very little!

Working Dogs

Today, working dogs help people in much the same way as they have always done. They are bred to do jobs such as herding and protecting animals, guarding people and their property, or pulling heavy loads. In recent years, people have found even more ways for dogs to help them. For example, Labrador retrievers are trained as guide dogs for the blind, and Newfoundlands rescue people from drowning.

Working dogs are intelligent, quick to learn, loyal, and affectionate. These characteristics make them very good companions. Many are also large and strong, so they might be unsuitable for some families, especially those with a small home. A Great Dane grows to about 30 inches (76 cm) tall at the shoulders. And if these dogs are not properly trained, they can get into all sorts of trouble—such as diving into a lake to "rescue" swimmers who don't need rescuing!

Strength and endurance make husky dogs ideal for pulling sleds.

21

Poodles were bred from retrievers. The way in which a poodle's coat is shaved and cut is called a clip.

Nonsporting Dogs

From the spotted Dalmatian to the shaggy Lhasa apso, nonsporting dogs vary in size, coat, color, and personality. Many nonsporting breeds were bred from sporting or working dogs, but today most are valued as pets or show dogs.

Some nonsporting breeds of dogs, such as the schipperke (SKI-PUR-KEE), are a rare sight in most neighborhoods. Others, like the poodle—that sometimes look like neatly clipped hedges after having had their coat trimmed—are more easily recognized. Poodles belong to more than one group of dogs because they come in different sizes. Standard poodles, which are the biggest type of poodle, and miniature poodles are nonsporting dogs. Despite their name, miniature poodles are not the smallest type of poodle. Toy poodles—a type of toy dog—are the smallest!

Bulldogs were once fierce fighting dogs. But today they are classed as nonsporting dogs. Today's bulldogs are friendly and have had their aggression bred out of them.

Herding Dogs

All types of herding dogs share one very special skill. They are all experts at moving large numbers of other animals, such as sheep, cattle, or goats, from one place to another. Not all herding dogs are big like the Old English sheepdog. A corgi is only about 1 foot (30 cm) tall at the shoulders. However, it can move a large herd of cows by running around the animals nipping at their heels!

Many herding dogs are now household pets because they make wonderful companions and enjoy being trained. Most herding dogs never get to herd other animals, but the **instinct** to do so has stayed with them. Dogs that attack sheep or cattle risk being shot at by an angry farmer. Therefore, to prevent these dogs from getting into trouble, owners should keep herding dogs on a leash when walking them near a group of other animals—even ducks or swans.

A Friend for Life

If you are thinking about getting a pet dog, there are some important things to consider. It will need care and attention for its whole life. Big dogs, such as Great Danes, might only live for eight or nine years, but small ones, such as pugs, may live up to 16 years. Some terriers might reach 20 years. An Australian sheepdog holds the "long-life" record at 29 years and five months!

No matter how long a dog lives, it is the quality of its life that is important. Dogs need food, exercise, love, and comfort every day. They also need **veterinary** checkups and medical care.

Choosing the right kind of dog can be difficult. It is important to have one that fits in well with the whole family. Whatever kind of dog you choose, caring for it is hard work. But these daily "chores" do not usually take long, and they are normally a lot of fun for everyone—especially the dog!

Friendly and energetic, the golden retriever is a very popular pet breed. Golden retrievers are often trained as guide dogs for blind people.

27

Puppy Love

A female dog usually has a litter of young, called **puppies**. An average litter has six puppies, but they can have anywhere from 1 to 12 puppies. The puppies are born blind and deaf. Just like human babies, puppies sleep most of the time. They open their eyes and ears when they are about two weeks old. After about three weeks, they can wag their tails and bark.

Puppies drink only their mother's milk until they are three to five weeks old. Then **weaning** begins, and they can start eating special puppy food. A puppy is fully weaned and ready to leave its mother at six to eight weeks old.

When choosing a new puppy from a litter, make sure it is healthy. It should be active and aware of everything around it. It should have a shiny coat, bright eyes, and clean ears. In addition, before you take your new puppy home, you need to buy a dog bed, toys, food bowls, and a collar and leash.

The milk that the mother dog supplies has all the right nutrients to help puppies grow fast.

A puppy will play
with and chew almost
anything—including
its owner's homework!

Making Friends

A new dog owner needs to make his or her pet welcome, so the dog will feel like part of the family. The dog will probably feel scared or homesick and will need time to adjust to its new home. The dog will need to feel safe and comfortable during these first few days of transition. It should be given a quiet corner of its own, where it can find its bed, with food and water in the same room, too.

Show your new friend to its corner and allow it to get settled for a while. It is a good idea to give the dog something with a familiar scent on it, such as a blanket or a soft toy, from its previous home. Once the dog feels comfortable, slowly introduce it to any other pets in the house one at a time.

Who's in Charge?

When a dog has settled into its new home, it will want to know who is in charge. In the wild, a dog belongs to a **pack**—a group of dogs with one leader, or **dominant** dog. Once your dog realizes that it is not the leader of its new "pack," it will happily let you take charge. However, you must be firm but kind and not betray its trust.

Dog owners should also be thoughtful of other people. They should keep their dog on a leash in public places. This will prevent the dog from being a nuisance or running into the street and causing an accident. There are "leash laws" in some communities. There are also "pooper scooper" laws, which mean that dog owners must clean up their dog's mess from the street.

Dogs need to be trained so that they behave themselves at home and outside. That can be fun for both dog and owner. A happy dog is a well-trained one. It should learn to come when called, sit, lie down, and stay. It should also be taught to heel when walking, to prevent it from pulling on the leash and taking its owner for a walk!

Like their ancestors, the wolves, pet dogs are happy to be in a group, or "pack."

33

Dogs prefer their bed to
be somewhere quiet away
from noise and drafts.

House-training

One of the first things a new puppy needs is house-training. At first, it will relieve itself on the floor. But it should never be punished for that. It might take about 12 weeks to fully house-train a puppy. Until then, it is a good idea to keep it confined to one area, such as the kitchen.

You can take your puppy in the backyard to relieve itself. It is best to do that when it wakes up and after its meals. At night, or if you go out, you can cover the floor with newspaper. Puppies prefer to relieve themselves on paper. You can gradually decrease the amount of paper. The puppy soon learns to wait until it is outside to relieve itself.

Dogs love to go for walks. The best time is first thing in the morning and about half an hour after a meal. A final walk at bedtime is a good idea, too. You should always remember to take the "pooper scooper" to clean up after your dog!

A Visit to the Vet

A veterinarian, or vet, is an animal doctor.
All new pet dogs, especially puppies, should
be taken to a vet for a checkup. To help keep
them healthy, dogs need regular checkups.

The vet gives dogs **vaccinations** to protect
them from diseases. Dogs are vaccinated regularly
against diseases such as canine distemper, rabies,
and hepatitis. Puppies need to be vaccinated
before they come into contact with other dogs.
Rabies is very dangerous and can be transmitted
through the bite of an infected animal. It also
affects people. Anyone bitten by a dog with
rabies should seek medical attention right away.

The vet might give medicines to prevent or
treat **parasites**, such as fleas and worms. Fleas
live in a dog's fur. They bite the skin, causing
sores and irritation. All dogs, especially puppies,
need to be "dewormed" regularly. Worms can
make dogs sick, and can be passed to people
through dog feces.

Sometimes, a vet will **neuter** a dog to prevent
it from having or fathering unwanted puppies.

When a dog is ill, it sometimes becomes less active. It might eat less or even stop eating altogether. Owners should take their dog to the vet for a checkup if those or other changes in its habits are noticed.

A Chinese crested dog has its dinner.

Favorite Foods

Dogs need more than just meat to keep them healthy. Other foods, including fish, cereals, and certain fruits and vegetables, are also good for them. Manufactured dog food, which comes in wet or dry forms, contains all the nutrients a dog needs. Puppies should be given special puppy food that has all the right nutrients to help them grow strong and remain healthy.

Big dogs need far more food than small ones. A Great Dane eats about eight times as much as a Chihuahua. Adult dogs normally eat just one meal a day. However, puppies need four small meals a day until they are three months old, then two meals until they reach six months of age.

Dogs can also be given the occasional dog treat. However, a pet dog should not be given too many treats or too much "human food" because it will soon become overweight and unhealthy. In addition, certain human foods are poisonous for dogs. These foods include grapes, raisins, onions, macadamia nuts, and chocolate.

In the Doghouse

Some dogs, especially working dogs, are usually kept outside in special doghouses. It is important to make sure that the doghouse provides shelter from both cold and hot weather and does not get damp. The old saying "in the doghouse" refers to someone who is in trouble and at risk of having to sleep outside with the dogs!

Many dogs share the family home. Given the choice, most pet dogs would prefer to sleep on the couch, or even in a bed! They should, however, have a place of their own where they can relax and sleep without being disturbed.

A cardboard box with newspaper and old towels is fine for puppies. It can be replaced quickly and cheaply if the puppy chews it or if the puppy relieves itself on it. Proper dog beds are best for adult dogs. They come in a range of sizes and shapes, and include rigid plastic beds, wicker baskets, and beanbags. All dog beds should be cleaned regularly.

A pair of guard dogs shares a doghouse, or kennel. Dogs like to rest or sleep up to 14 hours each day.

A Saint Bernard pants appreciatively as its owner grooms its head.

Keeping Clean

Regular **grooming** keeps a dog looking and feeling good. Dogs groom themselves by licking and nibbling their fur. Many dog breeds, however, have come to rely on humans for grooming. Most dogs enjoy being groomed if it is done properly and does not cause discomfort. Grooming mostly involves brushing the coat—unless, of course, the dog is a hairless breed! Different dog brushes are available for each type of coat.

Dogs also need their teeth and claws checked. If the claws are too long, a vet should clip them. Hard biscuits or rawhide chews help keep dogs' teeth clean, but it is better to brush their teeth using a soft brush and special toothpaste from the vet. Cleaning dogs' teeth when they are puppies helps get them used to toothbrushes.

A dirty, smelly dog always needs a bath. However, for regular maintenance, once or twice a year is usually enough. It is important to use special dog shampoos. Dry shampoo is a powder that removes oil from the dog's coat. It is dusted in and then brushed out.

Fun and Games

Puppies love to play. Play is important because it helps puppies develop and stops them from becoming bored. Because its owner will not always be around to play with it, a puppy needs to learn to play by itself. If a puppy has its own toys, it will not look for something to chew, like its owner's best pair of shoes! A wide range of special toys is available. Older dogs like toys, too. Owners should never use sticks or stones as toys because they can injure a dog. All dogs love to fetch or catch a ball, but anything smaller than a tennis ball might get stuck in a dog's throat.

Dogs also enjoy games such as tug-of-war. In games like that, dogs are showing their wild side. They are trying to be dominant. It is best not to let a boisterous, confident dog win all the time. But it might help to let a shy, timid dog win sometimes. When two dogs play together, one might roll over on its back and "give in." The dog is being **submissive** and allowing the other dog to be dominant.

Play creates a bond between dog and owner. A dog might bring a toy to its owner and "ask" to play.

45

The Samoyed originates
from Siberia, in Russia.
This agile breed was
originally developed
to herd caribou.

Showing Off

Many dog owners like to enter their dogs in shows and competitions. In these shows, experts judge a dog on how it looks, how it moves, and its temperament, or nature. Many communities hold local dog competitions, but the **American Kennel Club** supervises most pedigree dog competitions across the United States.

Dogs can compete in three kinds of competitions. They can enter a dog show, an obedience trial, or a field trial. Judges at a dog show check to see if a dog is typical of its breed. The best example of a certain breed wins a "best in show" award. Obedience trials judge dogs on their behavior. The dogs must recognize and obey hand signals or commands. In field trials, a dog pretends to hunt and shows the judges how well it can find or retrieve "prey."

Dog Stars

Since the start of film, television, and radio, dogs have been entertaining people with their skills. Many have become famous "actors." Three of them have even been awarded a star on Hollywood's "Walk of Fame."

Strongheart and Rin Tin Tin were German Shepherds that appeared in silent movies in the 1920s. Rin Tin Tin also starred on the radio, doing his own sound effects!

Lassie was a character in a 1940 novel. The book was first made into a movie in 1943. The dog that starred in it was a rough collie named Pal. Pal's descendants play the part of Lassie in movies today.

Dogs are not really actors. They are specially trained to perform tricks in front of a camera. They have a team of handlers and trainers. Being a dog star is hard work. When a dog star gets tired, it has other dogs that look just like it to act as doubles. But whether dog star, stand-in, purebred champion, or plain old mutt, all pet dogs are equally special animals!

Words to Know

American Kennel club Founded in 1884, the organization that registers dog breeds in the United States and oversees dog shows and trials.

Ancestors Early types of an existing species.

Breeds Types of purebred, or pedigree, dogs.

Crossbreeds Dogs that have parents of different breeds.

Domestic Tamed and bred by humans.

Dominant Having control over a group.

Flush To chase prey out of their hiding places.

Grooming Cleaning or brushing fur.

Instinct Anything that an animal does naturally.

Mammals Animals that have hair and feed their young on milk.

Mongrels Dogs whose parents are not purebred, and whose family tree cannot be traced.

Neuter	To perform an operation on a dog to prevent it from having puppies.
Pack	Animals that live and hunt together as a group.
Parasites	Tiny creatures that live on, or in, an animal and feed off it.
Pedigree	A dog whose ancestors are purebred, and whose family tree can be traced.
Prey	An animal hunted or caught by another, usually to eat.
Puppies	Young dogs.
Registered	A dog that is recognized as purebred by a kennel club.
Submissive	Allowing others to take control.
Track	To follow using sight, smell, or hearing.
Vaccinations	Injections given to protect against diseases, mainly infectious diseases.
Veterinary	Animal medical care carried out by a veterinarian, or animal doctor.
Weaning	The gradual replacement of the mother's milk by solid food.

Find Out More

Books

Crisp, M. *Everything Dog: What Kids Really Want to Know About Dogs.* Kids' FAQs. Minnetonka, Minnesota: NorthWord Books for Young Readers, 2003.

Kehret, P. *Shelter Dogs: Amazing Stories of Adopted Strays.* Morton Grove, Illinois: Albert Whitman & Company, 2003.

Web sites

American Kennel Club: Activity Sheets for Children
www.akc.org/public_education/resources.cfm?page=7
Tons of information about responsible dog ownership.

Dog Printouts
www.enchantedlearning.com/subjects/mammals/dog/
A lot of pictures of dogs to print and color in.

Index

A, B, C

Airedale 16

American Kennel Club 47

barking 15, 28

basenji 14, 15

basset hound 5

birth 28

bloodhound 15

Boston terrier 16

breeds 5, 11

bull terrier 16

bulldog 23

Chihuahua 8, 18, 39

Chinese crested dog 38

coat 22, 23, 28, 43

corgi 24

D, E, G

Dalmatian 23

diseases 36

ears 28

eyes 15, 28

golden retriever 27

Great Dane 20, 25, 39

grooming 42, 43

guard dogs 16, 41

guide dogs 20, 27

H, L, M

height 16, 18, 20

herding 5, 7, 11, 20, 24, 46

hounds 11, 15

house-training 35

hunting 7, 12, 15

husky 8, 9, 21

Labradoodle 11

Labrador retriever 11, 20

Leonburger 10

Lhasa apso 23

mongrels 11

N, O, P

Newfoundland 10, 20

nonsporting dogs 11, 23

nose 12, 15

Old English sheepdog 24

pack 32, 33

pedigree 11

play 30, 44, 45

pointers 12

poodles 8, 11, 19, 22, 23

pugs 19, 25

puppies 28, 29, 30, 35, 36,
    39, 43, 44

Pyrenean mountain dog 10

R, S, T

rescue dogs 7, 20

retrievers 12, 13, 22

rough collie 48

Saint Bernard 10, 42

Samoyed 46

scent hounds 15

Schipperke 23

setters 12

sheepdogs 6, 25

Siberian husky 8

sight hounds 15

sleep 28, 41

sniffer dogs 7

spaniel 12

sporting dogs 11, 12, 23

terriers 11, 16, 25

toy dogs 11, 19

V, W, Y

veterinary check 25, 36, 37

walking 24, 32, 33, 35

weight 14, 19

wolves 8, 33

working dogs 11, 20,
    23, 40

Yorkshire terrier 17